THROUGH
Sickness &
HEALTH

JOHN & DEBRA BURNS

Copyright © 2021 John and Debra Burns.
All rights reserved. No part of this book may be reproduced, scanned,
or distributed in any printed or electronic form without permission.
First Edition: June 2021
Printed in the United States of America

Table of Contents

Foreword i

Introduction 1

Preparing for the Wedding 3

The First Three Years of Our Marriage 6

Breast Cancer 8

John's Eyesight 20

The Power of Agreement 23

John's Next Test 26

Breast Cancer for the Third Time 28

Testimonies of Other Couples 31

End Your Journey In Victory 46

Scriptures of Encouragement 48

Foreword

As you read this book, it is imperative to be mindful that many of us have either seen or experienced sickness firsthand. It may not be easy for one to remember their own perilous time of going through the process of healing, so it should not be taken lightly that John and Debra have decided to share intimate and private details of their own illnesses with you as a way to show you how mighty the power of God that they serve is. One thing I can say for certain about this strong and faithful man and woman of God is that they are a true testament to the *power of healing and God's ability to do exceedingly and abundantly*. Both Debra and John exemplify how to walk by faith and not by sight (Hebrews 11:1). They held each other up through every unforeseen situation, and honored their marital vows through sickness and in health.

I have witnessed both of these individuals trust God through every sickness that ever tried to come upon them. I have seen them persevere no matter what the medical report stated. Witnessing Debra overcome cancer multiple times as a survivor encouraged me to *never* underestimate the power of God.

Undoubtedly, this book will enlighten you about *true* faith. It will show you that God's power is alive and well. It will inspire you to **walk by faith and not by sight.** It will show you that God is indeed a miracle worker. You will find yourself asking *how does one accrue such enormous faith?* You will read this book in awe of how John, a living, breathing and walking example of courage, continued in his business with the challenges of an amputation, diabetes, near blindness and COVID-19.

This book will demonstrate how Debra continued with her calling in ministry as a prophetess, author, and teacher of the Gospel. Debra managed to stay focused and show such remarkable resilience as she completed her bachelor's and master's degree in the midst of battling breast cancer and near kidney failure. She walks in grace (always remaining eloquently dressed) despite having a double mastectomy. Not even that could hold her back or keep her down.

I personally witnessed both of them get up from their bed of affliction, so that they could worship and serve the Lord *every* Sunday while enduring hospitalizations and complications of COVID-19. Not even a pandemic could stop John from running his business or Debra from progressing with her multitude of accomplishments. God certainly proved himself strong in the lives of this mighty couple.

It is with honor I write my support of this book to implore, encourage, and inspire others seeking to overcome personal obstacles. It is not always about *what* you go through, but *how* you get through. John and Debra's lives truly exemplify overcoming obstacles, and how to love and care for your spouse no matter the unfortunate circumstances. I leave you with this nugget that John speaks over his wife and his family when challenges arise, "Trust God."

Shorlanda Mason
Proprietor and Education Consultant

Foreword

In a culture where the entity and sacredness of the marriage covenant is being diluted, the testimony of John and Debra Burns is a heartfelt reminder to the world of what it means to live out your marriage vows. *Through Sickness and Health* is a beautiful illustration of faith, the power of agreement, endurance, resilience, grace and God's healing power.

The trials they've experienced throughout their marriage is a witness to God's essential nature, character, and ultimately to the saving work of Jesus Christ. As you read their testimony of marriage triumph and travail, I pray your heart is ignited with greater zeal and love for marriage.

Dr. E Blessing Utti
Quality Life Contract Rehabilitation

Introduction

"Be completely humble and gentle; be patient, bearing with one another in love. Make every effort to keep the unity of the Spirit through the bond of peace."

\- Ephesians 4:2-3 (NIV)

My husband and I are so excited to share our experience about how we made it through some health challenges as a married couple; and the importance of encouraging one another through that journey. As we navigated those tough seasons, we both realized that our marriage vows to each other were not just for happy days when everything is going fine, but that they must also hold true even in the toughest of times. As we encountered much, we remembered how we had both confessed before our guests and before God this declaration, *"For better or worse, for richer or for poorer, in sickness and health, until death do us part."*

We pray that this book is an encouragement to couples. Know that as a couple you can come out victoriously and you can love each other through it all unconditionally, through Christ our Lord.

Please also know that in no way are we glorifying sickness, but what we are emphasizing is that as couples walk together in agreement, God will show Himself strong in this area as well. Whatever you may be going through, know this, God can restore.

Much Love,

John and Debra Burns

Preparing for the Wedding

"That is why a man leaves his father and mother and is united to his wife, and they become one flesh."
— Genesis 2:24 (NIV)

From the perspective of the woman, preparation for the wedding is one of the most exciting times. You excitedly tell everyone you are engaged to get married and show off your engagement ring. You talk with friends you want to be a part of your bridal party as a maid of honor, bridesmaid, flower girl or ring boy; and you busy yourself finding a venue, décor and much, much more! In my case, I spent eight months spending a lot of money on this memorable event. I remember running here and there looking for the right colors and the perfect wedding dress that would fit our budget. I was honored to be getting married, but believe me the preparation can be very emotional. Even with those emotions, I was still excited to become the wife of John Burns II. During this time my fiancé John, who is now my husband, let me do the most. He wanted anything and everything that would make me happy.

As we prepared for our wedding day, all we talked about was how we wanted to spend the rest of our lives together. It was these types of talks that helped ease the pain of spending a lot of money for our wedding day. Getting wedding invitations, favors for the tables, and decorations was no joke! We would look each other in the eyes and say, "It's worth it all."

As we planned our wedding, we didn't spend much time talking about how we would handle difficult situations that might arise within our marriage. We just focused on thinking that everything would be pollyanna and excessively sweet. The reality of the matter is that many marriages fail because they only prepare for one day and that day is the wedding day.

Like John and I, the conversation between most couples never considers real life intervening on all those pleasant plans. Marriage shouldn't be taken lightly. For many couples, after the wedding day they soon discover that cohabitating is not that easy.

Years of marriage have given John and I a clear understanding that true marriage takes work.

Situations that happened to both of us caused us to realize why we got married in the first place. *Until death do us part* takes much work. It isn't just a cliché that was added into our vows.

When it comes to Christian counseling, oftentimes discussions about what if situations never come up. Engaged couples are not given much advice about how to make it through the rough times that will inevitably come or told that the marriage is never solid no matter how many years they have been married. This is why many marriages end in divorce within the first five years. But that won't be your story. I pray that you will have those *what-if* conversations more sooner than later, and that you would be inspired by our testimony to navigate any challenges that might arise within your marriage.

Fun Fact:

Did you know ten states in the U.S. mandate premarital counseling prior to getting married? All the states that require premarital counseling have lower divorce rates.

The First Three Years of Our Marriage

"There is a time for everything, and a season for every activity under the heavens." — Ephesians 3 :1 (NIV)

The first three years of our marriage felt like we were still on our honeymoon. I can remember running home after work everyday to see John, and he would do the same. Not being a great cook, I still cooked what I knew how to cook, which wasn't much, but I did enjoy doing it for him. I want to share that John came from a family of cooks, so in that area I was a step down. *Laugh with me.* Inspite of this, John loved it and he ate it all. This is the stage where you think your spouse is perfect, and both of you are having fun.

Within those first few years, we were so excited to move from my home that I had brought on my own into a condo we purchased together. Things were still going great. Both of us were doing well in our professions, finances were going well, and we were both healthy. On top of this, we both loved the Lord, and we had a great blended family. We never looked at our children as stepchildren, but as blended.

While some couples have problems with sharing their bank accounts, not us. We enjoyed putting our resources together for the betterment of our relationship. Please note that this didn't mean we never had any disagreements on where we spent the money.

Those first few years of marriage were our puppy love stage. This was the stage where I would find myself waking up before him, making sure my hair was combed and putting on my make-up. Sorry to say I am now a slacker in this area. In speaking with other newlyweds, I found out many women followed my same routine.

Well, this was the first three years of marriage for us. You will see in the next chapter our first big challenge together.

Breast Cancer

"For all the promises of God in Him are yea, and in Him Amen, unto the glory of God by us."
— 2 Corinthians 1:20 (KJV)

It was the end of 2006, and I was having my yearly mammogram. As a breast cancer survivor, having an annual mammogram was normal for me. I had first been diagnosed eight years prior in 1998, so since that time, after having my first surgery, my mammogram testing always went well. In fact, I always looked forward to giving my testimony about how I was an overcomer.

This time of the year wasn't any different for me. I knew that I would receive a good report from my doctor. I was so excited that I was eight years totally free from breast cancer. I said to myself that I had done my self-care and treatments, and prayed, so I was fine.

A few days after my exam, I got a call from my doctor stating that he wanted me to come back for more testing. I asked why. He shared that he had seen some tumors that weren't there previously, and he just needed to make sure. Well, that didn't faze me because this usually happens. I said to myself, "Not much could have changed within a year, so why not?"

The additional testing included another 3D mammogram, which according to the Mayo Clinic, is an imaging test that combines multiple breast X-rays to create a three- dimensional picture of the breast. I also had to do a breast biopsy, which is a procedure where they remove a small sample of the breast tissue that allows doctors to determine if what they see is cancerous.

After a few days passed, I got another call. I still remember the voice of the doctor, which was deep. I could tell in his voice that he needed my full attention. The conversation went something like this. "This is doctor so and so, can you and your husband come to my office?" My question to him was, "Why?" He replied, "It is very important." As I held the phone, I looked at John with tears in my eyes. He looked at me asking, "What honey, what?"

Ending the conversation with my doctor, I told John that the phone call was a repeat of the conversation I had with my doctor in 1998, asking me to come to his office immediately.

John grabbed me, held me tight and said, "Know this honey, whatever it is I am here with you. I love you much." These words were so powerful to me. What John shared with me in that moment also connected to the Word of God.

"I am here with you through all times."
\- Matthew 28:20

This interaction between John and I also reflected how marriage is a shadow of the covenant we have with Christ. God has made an oath with us as believers to never leave us.

As we drove to the doctor's office, I looked out the window the entire time because I didn't want John to see me cry. Thank God for His voice. I could clearly hear God say, "I did it before, I will do it again."

As we entered the doctor's office, the look on the doctor's face said it all. It was like I could hear his

Through Sickness and Health

thoughts regarding my situation before he said anything. Looking at the doctor I could see that his gestures, facial expressions and eye contact said it all.

The doctor asked John and me to have a seat. Let me just say while he was talking, everything seemed to be moving in slow motion. Those few seconds seemed to be 10 to 15 minutes.

As we listened intensely, that's when he hit us with the news that the cancer had come back in the same place. In that moment, all I could do was stare at him. As he gave me my diagnosis, I continued to stare. At one point I thought I was speaking, but then I realized nothing was coming out. I eventually realized that the doctor and my husband were waiting for me to respond. I took a few breaths and said, "Please tell me my next step." Mind you, as all of this is going on I could hear my husband whispering real low, "Lord have mercy," and, "Honey, by His stripes you are healed."

The doctor suggested that since the cancer had come back a second time, I should have my left breast removed, a mastectomy. For those who are not aware of what a mastectomy is I will explain.

A mastectomy is a surgical operation to remove a breast. This is a procedure to remove all breast tissue from a breast to treat or prevent breast cancer. My first go round I had a lumpectomy, which involved removing the tumor from the breast.

As the doctor suggested this, in my mind I am thinking he must have the wrong person. As he continued to talk, I realized no, it was me he was talking to. Through tears I managed to tell him that I wanted a second option. To my surprise he agreed. In the emotional state that I was in I could still hear the sweet voice of my husband saying, "Honey, we are going to conquer this together." I could also hear the Lord saying, "This sickness isn't unto death."

The next day I made an appointment with my oncologist. I thought for sure she would give me another way to treat this without having a mastectomy. "Truly," I said, "She would give me other medications that would make it go away." Well, that didn't happen. My oncologist agreed with the doctor in saying that since it had come back at the next stage, that it was time to remove it. After hearing this, the tears just wouldn't stop falling. I looked my husband in his eyes; and at this point he took me in his arms and said, "Baby, all is well."

My thoughts began to race. I knew I didn't want to die, and I struggled with how I would explain this to my girls. On our way home, there wasn't much conversation between John and I. John drove, while I stared out the window asking myself, "Why this again?"

This went on for a few days. My words were few, and so were John's. I could see that he didn't want anything to upset me, so he walked light. I could also tell that he was praying for me.

After a few more days passed, because of John's prayers and him loving on me, and me silently praying, I got out of my pity party. I began to hear the voice of the Lord say, "This sickness isn't unto death.

"When he heard this, Jesus said, "This sickness will not end in death. No, it is for God's glory so that God's Son may be glorified through it." - John 11:4

As the Lord was ministering this to me, John came to me and said the same thing. This let me know that God had us on His mind, so I said, "Lord I believe, help my unbelief."

"Immediately the father of the child cried out and said with tears, "Lord, I believe, help my unbelief.""
- Mark 9:24 (NKJV)

Because I was diagnosed at the end of 2006, the doctor said we would wait until January 5, 2007 to have the surgery. The enemy tried to make me afraid, but I could still hear the Lord saying, "This sickness isn't unto death." I could also hear my husband saying the same thing.

Being in this place was hard for me. It was hard for John as well. We had only been married for three years, and we were both still getting to know each other, along with our children. John's conversation with the Lord was, "Lord I know that you will not take my new wife and leave me here with the children without their mother. Lord I finally found the *love of my life*, please don't do this."

It was at this point that the Lord spoke to him saying the same thing, "This sickness isn't unto

Through Sickness and Health

death." Please note that this scripture is also found in John 11:4 (NLT). It reads, "But when Jesus heard about it he said, "Lazarus's sickness will not end in death." No, it happened for the glory of God so that the Son of God will receive glory from this."

My husband and I got the revelation that just as Lazarus' sickness was not unto death, neither would mine be. *"I will live and see the salvation of the Lord,"* was our daily confession. John and I both believed that death would not be my final result.

"For to me, to live is Christ and to die is gain."
- Philippians 1:21 (NIV)

Let us encourage your hearts as believers. We are winners either way. As you read our story, don't in any way think if you had someone go home to be with the Lord, that God didn't answer your prayers. As a believer they still gained. It could be that person completed their purpose and now they are in the presence of the Lord with a new body.

When you look at John 4:11 it also mentions, "So that the Son of God might be glorified." The purpose was not only that I WOULD live, but also

15

that the Son of God might be glorified. My sickness of breast cancer would accomplish the glory of God. In that very hour, God's healing power was at work in my life. The glory of God in my life was God displaying His working power of a miracle. Let me encourage your hearts. Jesus came to heal all manner of disease.

One of our favorite scriptures is found in Isaiah 53:5 (KJV). It reads, *"But he was wounded for our transgressions; he was bruised for our iniquities: the chastisement of our peace was upon him; and with his stripes we are healed."*

I went through my second surgery on January 7th, and you got it, I am still here! God did it again! As I think about my healing from cancer the second time, I am reminded of a story in the Bible that blesses me every time I read it. It is about how God healed the man who was born blind. The man's name was Celidonius at Siloam. In your spare time read John 9:1-41, which talks about this miracle. This story reminds me of myself because people had the same questions for me as the disciples had in the second verse of chapter 9.

Through Sickness and Health

"And his disciples asked him, "Rabbi, who sinned, this man or his parents? It was said that I must be living in sin or I must be living in unforgiveness. Jesus advised the disciples that it was none of these things."

- John 9:2 (ESV)

I so loved the next answer that Jesus gave to his disciples in John 9:3 (ESV). *"Jesus stated, "Neither this man nor his parents sinned, but this happened so the work of God might be displayed in his life.""*

Let me encourage you. When you go through something, whether it be sickness, the loss of a loved one or anything else, please get it out of your mind that it is a punishment from God. It is not, it is so that His healing power can be displayed in your life and that the glory of God is manifested. This is a good place to shout! I also believe this may be a time where many may try to disgrace you or misjudge you. Your overcoming sickness may cause a change in the heart of people who make or have made false claims.

As you continue reading John 9, you will see that the man is healed. You will also see that many people didn't believe he was the same man that had been born blind. He said, "Yes, it is me. I can see."

They asked who did it, and he answered and said a man called Jesus. Here he gives God the glory. The interesting thing is that the man didn't know very much about Jesus, but he did know that He was his healer. Let me say this. You may not be a Bible scholar, in the five- fold ministry or saved for many years, but know that Jesus is the healer.

The man also said, "All I know is I was blind, but now I can see." This was his profound testimony. When God says that He wants to do something in your life so that His Glory may be manifested in you, you can take His word to the bank. God's splendor was displayed through the man receiving his sight. God released His super abundance of grace and goodness within his life.

Let's look at the word glory for a minute. The Hebrew word for glory is "kabod," which means weight; heft; heaviness; worth. What God wants for his children is to be part of displaying His glory within your life. What we see here with the man who was blind is God fulfilling His promise in his life. It is important for us to understand that the promises of God are yes and Amen.

John

Being her husband, I understood the only way to get through this was to keep my eyes towards the hills, as I realized that my help comes from the Lord. Even as I continued to encourage my wife daily, I first had to encourage myself by confessing the Word of God daily over the situation. I was reminded that He that keeps Israel never slumbers or sleeps.

John's Eyesight

"I will lift up mine eyes unto the hills, from whence cometh my help. My help cometh from the Lord, which made heaven and earth." – Psalm 121:1-2 (KJV)

Four years had passed, and we made it through breast cancer. We had overcome that hurdle, but we didn't know what was ahead of us. It was in 2011 that John realized he was having problems with his eyesight. In the beginning we didn't think much about it, and just thought that maybe he needed to get his eye prescription updated. During this time, we also noticed that John had begun to be involved in more car accidents, so the family at this point became very concerned. So, within a few days of noticing his eyesight getting worse, John made an appointment to see an optometrist.

The next week John went to the optometrist and the doctor explained that he had retinal detachment in his eyes. This explained the problems he had been having with his eyesight. A retinal detachment is when the tissue at the back of the eye pulls away from a layer of blood vessels that provide necessary oxygen and nourishment to the eyes. As you can see this was very serious.

I just love the level of faith that my husband walks in. Below John will share what he went through.

John

When I heard the optometrist confirm what was going on with me, I immediately understood what Debra had gone through after being diagnosed with breast cancer for the second time. I told the doctor, "You must have the wrong person, I just need a new prescription." In the past I had had laser surgery on my eyes, and that always worked. This time was a different story because the laser didn't work.

Being self -employed, and not being able to work, was a hard adjustment for me. I had never had to depend on anyone to take care for me, but I thank God for the support of my loving wife Debra. I can remember asking the doctor to just give me another eye exam. He showed me my results, which confirmed what was going on with my eyes. I thank God that my better half was there for me. Debra looked at me and reminded me that she was there for better or for worse and in sickness or health. I could hear her say, "Honey, many are the afflictions of the righteous, but the Lord delivers them out of them all (Psalm 34:19)."

I want to add this scripture is still very much a part of my life. I want to encourage someone right now. You may be in a situation or crisis where you don't see any light at the end of the tunnel, but I say unto you, "Our God is a God of the impossible." Know that your affliction is just for a short time. Know that there is hope even in the suffering. Let me add, I am back working, strong, and my business is going great. I am not driving currently, but I can say that I am still able to work and provide for my family. As I know that the Lord is the author and finisher of my faith, I know soon I will be behind the wheel again.

The word deliver in the Hebrew means to "snatch away" and "rescue". I prophesy that God is about to rescue you in Jesus name, so hold fast to His word. I want to end by sharing that my surgery went well. In this situation I again had to keep my eyes to the hills, which comes my help.

The Power of Agreement

"Can two walk together, except they be agreed?"
– Amos 3:3 (KJV)

How can two walk together unless they agree, is a question posed in Amos 3:3; but it must be a prevalent and real truth within a couple's life. When you are facing difficult situations, agreeing is a must. Please be careful of that third voice. What I mean by the third voice is the voice that tries to bring discord to your marriage. The power of agreement brings desired results. Walking together in agreement creates a strong marriage even in the roughest of times. I want to add that walking together in agreement is the will of God for all couples. I know that we are talking about sickness, but walking in agreement about everything concerning your marriage is a must as well.

Listed below are some scriptures on the power of agreement. Keeping that third voice out of your marriage, will also keep a hedge around your marriage. And the hedge will keep God in the midst of your marriage.

Matthew 18:19, "Again I say to you, if two of you agree on earth about anything they ask, it will be done for them by my father in heaven."

1 John 1:9, "If we confess our sins, he is faithful and just to forgive us our sins and to cleanse us from all unrighteousness."

1 John 5:14, "And this is the confidence that we have toward him, that if we ask anything according to his will he hears us."

John 14:14, "If you ask me anything in my name, I will do it."

1 Peter 5:7, "Casting all your anxieties on him, because he cares for you."

As you can see, God's Word backs up the word *agreement*. According to Strong's Concordance, the word agree in the Hebrew means to agree together.

Deuteronomy 32:30, "How could one chase a thousand and two put ten thousand to flight,

Through Sickness and Health

unless their Rock had sold them, and the Lord had surrendered them."

The power of agreement in prayer is a powerful tool for couples. Let's go to Matthew 18:19 which states, *"Again I say unto you, that if two of you shall agree on earth as touching anything that they shall ask, it shall be done for them of my Father which is in heaven."*

Jesus said that what you pray in agreement, His father will back up by answering your prayer. Jesus said it will be done by His Father in heaven. As long as your prayer lines up with the Word of God, it shall be answered. Agreement brings unity.

John's Next Test

"For we walk by faith, not by sight."
— 2 Corinthians 5:7 (KJV)

Now it is seven years later. We got over cancer for the second time and my eye surgery. Now we are in 2017. Some know that my profession is HVAC, which is heating, ventilation and air conditioning. I am a general contractor in this field. I was on a job working and I found myself stepping on a nail which caused me to get an infection in my right big toe. Because I didn't properly take care of the infection sooner, I found myself going to urgent care near our home. After the doctor examined my toe he said to me, "I'm sorry Mr. Burns, we need to amputate your big toe?" All I could say was, "Lord have mercy!" Immediately I was transferred to Ingalls Hospital in Harvey, Illinois. I thank God my wife was there to bring me encouragement. My surgery went well, however a few days later I was given another test to check the arteries in that right leg and to my surprise they were blocked. A surgeon met with me and Debra, and advised us that amputation of my right leg must be done below my knee. After I was given this news, I turned my head so Debra wouldn't see me cry. As soon as I turned my head Debra said to me, "Honey, God said I am here even in this and you will live to declare the works of the Lord and you will be a testimony to many." If I ever understood the verse, "I walk by faith and not by sight," I understood it even more during this time.

This was over three years ago, and praise be to God I am still here! I now have a prosthetic leg and I continue to work daily. If you didn't know I had a prosthetic leg, you wouldn't even know it. Now this is the power of God working His good pleasure in my life.

Breast Cancer
for the Third Time

"For all the promises of God in Him are Yes, and in Him Amen, to the glory of God through us."
— 2 Corinthians 1:20 (NKJV)

Just when I thought it was all over, another attack of that dreaded C word came back. Breast cancer struck again for the third time. Around November 15 of 2019, as usual I had my yearly mammogram. As I stated before, this was a norm for me. Before I start with this testimony, let me say this to the women, please get your yearly screening.

As I took the yearly mammogram, I said to myself, "I know all is well." Because I have fibrocystic breast, at times there is a thickening of the breast tissue that may be detected under the skin through an ultra-sound, biopsy or a 3D mammogram. Since many have fibrocystic breast, this is common among women. Many women have tumors or cysts that are not cancerous, so I believed this was the case for me.

Through Sickness and Health

A few days after taking all three breast exams, I received that call again. It was a repeat of the second time. As he had done before, my doctor asked that my husband and I come into his office. When John and I got to his office, the doctor had the same look on his face as the previous doctor had before. The only thing different about this this time, was that my doctor was a believer. As he released the diagnosis to me and John, he also gave me the Word of God. I felt the power of agreement so strong in his office. A threefold cord is not easily broken. I am referring to the verse located in Ecclesiastes 4:12, *"And if one can overpower him who is alone, two can resist him. A cord of three strands is not quickly torn apart."*

This is so powerful. The word three strands in Hebrew is mullahs, which means three. When three strands are twisted together the strands are stronger and are not easily broken like one strand would be. Let me prophetically say this. When you try to stand alone and isolate yourself from others, the attack is so much greater. The Word of God even says in James 5:14 (KJV), "Is any sick among you? Let him call for the elders of the church; and let them pray over him, anointing him with oil in the name of the Lord."

This is a sure recipe for answered prayers.

My surgery was on December 19, 2019; and God did it again for the third time. He delivered me. The healing power of God is so real. I am a living testimony. Please understand that the promises of God are yes and amen. God keeps His promises; and He never backs down from His Word. What you may think is impossible, is possible with our God.

John and I live by this verse daily, and it has been and is still evident in our lives.

"But He was wounded for our transgressions; He was bruised for our iniquities: the chastisement of our peace was upon him; and with His stripes we are healed."
- Isaiah 53:5 (KJV)

I am so amazed that even while we were going through, we were still able to bear fruit. It was only through the grace of God. Jesus took all our sickness on Him and took them to the cross.

Testimonies of Other Couples

The next few chapters will include testimonies of other couples who also stood the test of time. As you can see, through the power of agreement couples can overcome. I pray that their testimonies will encourage your heart to continue fighting the good fight of faith.

For Better or for Worse

It has been my pleasure to know Prophetess Debra for over 40 years. We have been there for each other in good times and bad. My husband and I are excited to share with her and her wonderful husband in this, her fifth book. They truly have a heart to encourage the Body of Christ.

For over 25 years my husband and I have had the privilege of personally ministering to married and engaged couples in retreats and workshops. God put on our heart that so many in the Body of Christ don't understand what they are saying when they say I do. We know we did not. As we prayed, sought God's face, and studied His Word, He began to show us marriage in the way He intended it to be in the beginning. God and his creation in fellowship together like in the garden before the fall. Marriage should be beautiful. It should be filled with two people who love God and each other. We have discovered with God at the head and godly works, it is truly doable.

As many couples have sat across our table, we always ask why they are there. If it is pre-marital

Through Sickness and Health

consulting they will say, "We fell in love," and if it is marital consulting they will say, "We fell out of love." Here is the truth. You may fall "in love," but it takes determination and godly works to stay in love. It does not just happen because you are meant to be together. It doesn't even happen if you know you were called to the ministry together. You must constantly work on it. One thing we know is that God loves covenant and marriage. In Isaiah 54:5 and Jeremiah 31:32, God calls himself Israel's husband.

> *"For thy Maker is thine husband; the Lord of hosts is his name…"* — Isaiah 54:5

> *"Not according to the covenant that I made with their fathers in the day that I took them by the hand to bring them out of the land of Egypt; which my covenant they brake, although I was an husband unto them, saith the Lord."* — *Jeremiah 31:32 (KJV)*

In Ephesians 5:25, men are instructed to love their wives as Christ loved the church. God desires to be ALL in our marriages, to help us succeed. He is not pleased when marriages don't give Him glory.

James 2:20 (KJV) says, "But wilt thou know, vain man that faith without works is dead." This is not a scripture that many would associate with marriage. We have been married for over 38 years. We can honestly say we have been on the highest mountain where everything was wonderful, and we have been in the lowest valley where just one off word would have sent one of us packing. But *doing* this scripture, yes I said *doing* this scripture, has brought our marriage back to where it pleases God. I don't care where your marriage is today. Grab hold to this scripture and do not let it go! Most people only quote, "Faith without works is dead." But the scripture in its entirety says, "But wilt thou know, O vain man, that faith without works is dead?" The Amplified Bible Classic (AMPC) version says it this way, "Are you willing to be shown proof you foolish (unproductive, spiritually deficient) fellow, that faith apart from (good) works is inactive, ineffective, and worthless?" Many marriages today are inactive, ineffective, worthless and some are just plain dead. You may be living in the same house, but not speaking, you may be sleeping in separate rooms, or the same room, but not touching. Everyone who knows you may think your marriage is perfect, but you hate to go home. You may even be praying

Through Sickness and Health

about your spouse. Some may be going or have gone to counseling. It seems to work for a while, but soon it is back to being inactive, ineffective and worthless...it appears dead. Let's pull out our spiritual defibrillator and put the paddles on the heart of our marriages and resuscitate them to new life in Christ.

Let God show you proof that your marriage can be resuscitated, active, effective, and worth it. We love when God says, "Let me prove to you my Word works." In the second part of this scripture He says "Vain, unproductive, or spiritually deficient man." You may say that is not me. I know my Bible and I know God, but in your marriage are you unproductive, spiritually deficient and vain. Let's put it in these simple words. Is what you are doing working? God says, "Try me!" He is saying to all of us who are trying to repair marriages in our own ability to give them to Him and do what He says, then watch Him change things. If you are complaining, going off, not speaking, being a doormat, cursing your mate out, or whatever you are doing that is not causing the change you are looking for, be honest, you are unproductive and spiritually deficient. Let's get serious, marriage needs faith in God! We MUST get a vision of what God wants in our marriage and hold on to that vision no matter what. There will be trials and difficulties in your marriage, but faith is seeing what God sees, believing what God believes and above all saying what God says about your marriage, your spouse and yourself.

Now let's talk about works. We can do *no works*, *bad works* or *good works*. Let's say you are a person that has always wanted to go to college. You have seen yourself graduating and walking across the stage. But you never apply for college after high school, you just sit at home waiting for a college to call and say you have been accepted. This is an example of faith with no works as described in James 2:20. Many couples can envision a better marriage, and desire a better marriage, but do nothing to get it.

Let's take that same scenario of someone who sees themselves graduating from college. That person gets up every day and goes to class, but instead of doing the work the professor assigns, they party, get high and drink, eventually dropping out of college. This person did bad works and received bad results. It is just like a marriage where you complain all the time that your spouse does nothing right, and before long your marriage is headed for divorce court.

God requires good works and good works are deliberate! God has a perfect plan, and it is not magic! God is not your genie granting all your wishes. God requires us to get in there with Him and do exactly what He tells us to do. John 6:63 explains what good works are. It says, "It is the spirit that quickeneth; the flesh profiteth nothing: the words that I speak unto you, they are spirit and they are life."

Let's pull this together; the Spirit gives life, effectiveness, and worth. Our flesh, emotions and feelings profit nothing. Do not get confused I did not say our emotions do not produce, they produce in abundance, but it does not profit. Profit means to be useful, beneficial, and better. Emotions can produce discord, anger, jealousy, envy and everything in Ephesians 4:31.

"Get rid of all bitterness, rage and anger, brawling and slander, along with every form of malice."
– Ephesians 4:31 (NIV)

Let's look at John 6:63 again. In a portion of the verse it says, "The Words that I (the Spirit of God) speak to YOU are spirit and life." What is God saying to you? What is He telling you to do? This requires time in prayer seeking God's direction.

This should be honest talking and listening to God. You maybe unsure of what God is saying. I can help you! It is everything you do not want to do, but hear God speaking in your heart. It is the thing that tells you to forgive, let go, give, have mercy, show grace, not be afraid to be hurt again, and to trust God yet again. Those things are Spirit and they are life.

In Genesis, God promises Abraham he would have a son with his wife Sarah at God's set time. Sarah became impatient, took matters into her own hands and encouraged Abraham to sleep with her bond woman, Hagar. He did, she got pregnant, and Ishmael was born. This caused all kinds of problems. In Genesis 12 Sarah tells Abraham to get rid of Hagar and Ishmael. Now look at Genesis 21:12 (KJV), "And God said unto Abraham, Let it not be grievous in thy sight because of the lad, and because of the bond woman; in all that Sarah hath said unto thee, hearken unto her voice; for in Isaac shall thy seed be called."

Abraham certainly had a right to be emotional; however, God literally told him to take control of his emotions. Sarah had encouraged this relationship. She made a mess of God's set time, and now she is telling him to put his oldest son out! According to verse 11 Abraham's emotions were very grievous. Grievous is defined here as sorrow and severe pain. God did not tell Abraham to do what He said. God told Him to do what Sarah said. The Word God gives directly to you, they are Spirit and they are life. The words God spoke to Abraham were difficult, but he had to move past his emotions to do what God said which was to listen to his wife. This was the same wife who had started the confusion, the wife that was not perfect, and the wife who was telling him to get rid of his oldest boy. However, Abraham did what God said and received abundant blessing for his obedience.

Allow God to tell you what to do with fears, hurt and unforgiveness before they produce death in your marriage. Begin to do the good works that will bring life back to your marriage. Marriages die every day out of anger, hurt, bitterness, selfishness, infidelity, and only seeing things your way because we do not want to do the good works. Let all of that go and let God prove His Word! We are not saying this will be easy. If it was easy, everyone would stay married, but we are a witness that if you put in the good works there is a profit that God promises.

What we are saying can be summed up in one scripture found in Luke 1:37 (KJV). It reads, "For with God nothing shall be impossible." My husband and I always say your case is not hopeless. Listen to the Spirit of God! Do the good works He is telling **YOU** to do and watch it bring life back into your marriage. If you apply the above principles, watch God work in sickness and health.

Ministers Raymond and Olivia Smith
Sword of the Spirit Ministries
Chicago, IL

In Sickness & In Health

Over the past 11 years, we have learned just what the sickness and health part of our marriage vows really means. My husband, a mighty man of faith, endurance and strength has been battling cancer for this amount of time. The Word tells us in 1 Corinthians 16:34, *"Give thanks unto the Lord; for he is good; for his mercy endureth forever."* When the diagnosis was given, of course giving God thanks was the furthest thing from our minds. Disappointment and fear crept in, but the Word of God rose up strong in us.

2 Timothy 1:7 says, *"God has not given a spirit of fear, but of power, love and a sound mind."*

This journey has increased our prayer life and we are believing God for the miracle of a total healing. Yes, we have gotten weary, worried and stressed, but we go back to a sound mind and we also stand on the scripture Isaiah 53:5, *"For he was wounded for our transgressions and bruised for our iniquities: the chastisement of our peace was upon him; and with his stripes we are healed."*

Seeing your loved one, your friend, your supporter, your confidant go through is not easy by any means, but I continue to stay encouraged and keep him encouraged. I remain his biggest cheerleader as we continue on this journey to healing. Dupree and I understand that daily we must devote ourselves to agreement and making sure our words line up with the Word of God. We understand that where there is unity, there is strength.

"God is our refuge and strength, a very present help in trouble." - Psalm 46:1

Elder Dupree and City Clerk Leslie Trimuel (Markham, IL)
Full Gospel Christian Assemblies International
Hazel Crest, IL

Til Death Do Us Part

One Monday afternoon in May 2011, my husband suffered a massive stroke while at work. He had been employed as a track inspector at a railroad for 32 years. He is a man who loved his job, and he was in great shape physically. He took no medication, and he had no health issues.

That stroke changed our lives forever! My husband lost the use of the left side of his body. He was subject to years of treatments including physical therapy, occupational therapy, and speech therapy. He still does not have full use of his left arm, YET! He can now open his left hand, however, he suffers from weakness on the left side, memory loss and speech delays.

When he began his climb back to life, some days I wanted to run away. I sometimes wanted to quit. His drive made me strong. He was determined to return to himself. I prayed earnestly from day one for his complete healing. Extensive therapy has brought him a long way. He is the father of two grown sons. We have had some bad days as well as some good. However, I constantly remind him of the good days and the goodness of our God. Many people very close to us have lost their lives to heart attacks, strokes and cancer, but he is still here! I remind him that God left him here for a reason. May 16, 2021 made ten years since he had the stroke.

Let me be honest. It has not been easy watching him daily. I assumed my role as his caregiver. Together we go to therapy, doctors' appointments and anywhere else he needs to go. I became a therapist, nurse, counselor, social worker, psychologist, speech pathologist, encourager, and anything else he needed me to be. One thing I was sure of, with God's help we could make it through this test as well. No, life is not the same, but it is our life together. We must press on for we are still standing! Thanks be to God who is our help and strength!

We celebrated 41 years of marriage in June of 2021. Look at God!

Through Sickness and Health

This is one of the scriptures I have leaned on. Isaiah 41:10 (GNB) which says, *"Do not be afraid. I am with you. I am your God. Let nothing terrify you. I will make you strong and help you; I will protect you and save you."*

Leonardo and Elder Matrie DeLeon
CTK Realty
Hazel Crest, IL

End Your Journey In Victory

John and I want to thank you for reading *Through Sickness and Health*. We pray that this book was a blessing and that your hearts were encouraged. Please note that we understand there will be times of weariness and fear, as well as times you may want to give up. In those times you must take hold of this verse, *"Casting down imaginations, and every high thing that exalteth itself against the knowledge of God,and bringing into captivity every thought to the obedience of Christ (2 Corinthians 10:5 (KJV))."*

As you and your spouse stand in agreement, let the Word of God become engrafted within your hearts. Let God's Word take root. To engraft means to join or fasten as if by grafting. The engrafted Word is able to save our souls.

John

Debra and I have shared some of the toughest times that we went through. We didn't share everything, but we shared enough to allow you to see and understand the importance of agreement and unity within a marriage. No matter what may come, you can navigate your journey in victory. Remember you are born of God, so you and your spouse have the power to walk and talk in agreement!

"Now to him who is able to do immeasurably more than all we ask or imagine according to his power that is at work within us." – Ephesians 3:20 (NIV)

As we stated at the beginning of this book, we are in no way glorifying illness. Our intention is to show you that unity in marriage will overcome everything. Remember, one can put a thousand to flight, and two can put ten thousand to flight.

Scriptures of Encouragement

We are ending this book with scriptures that you can read and confess today.

Matthew 18:19, "Again I say to you, if two of you agree on earth about anything they ask, it will be done for them by my Father in heaven."

Psalms 91:11, "For he shall give his angles charge over thee, to keep thee in all thy ways."

1 John 5:14, "This is the confidence we have in approaching God: that if we ask anything according to his will, he hears us."

Made in the USA
Columbia, SC
02 July 2021